How O

written by Pam Holden

How old are you?
When is your birthday?

birthday

How old will you be
on your birthday?

3

How old are your friends?

friends

Are your friends older or younger than you?

sisters

Do you have brothers and sisters?

Who is the oldest one
in your family?

Who is the youngest?

grandfather

Do you have a grandfather?
Is he very old?

grandmother

Do you have a grandmother?
How old is she?

How old is a baby?

Do you have some pets?
How old are they?

Who is the youngest
one in your class?

class

Who is the oldest?

The teacher is the oldest one in the class!